THE
NEW BABY

An activity book for soon-to-be
big brothers and sisters

Different animal babies have different names. Can you spot the babies of the following animals?

Giraffe, dog, fish, spider, pig, butterfly, crocodile, chicken, bear, kangaroo, weasel, rabbit, swan, horse, frog, llama, cat, sheep, deer...

kit

kitten

cygnet

caterpillar

calf

foal

cub

lamb

piglet

NAMES

kitten (yes, really!)

puppy

chick

What is your name?
What do you think baby's name
should be?

cria

hatchling

tadpole

fry

spiderling

fawn

joey

3 MONTHS

When baby is in mummy's tummy
it is called a fetus. At three
months, the fetus is the size
of a lemon and has hair on its
head and also fine hair all over
its body!

What colour is your hair?
Is it straight or is it curly?
Draw it here!

It takes nine months for a baby
to grow. That's three seasons.
Which season will it be when
the baby is born?

SPRING

SUMMER

AUTUMN

Colour this page in!

WINTER

Which season is
your birthday?

MY FAMILY

Which of these people look like
they come from your family?

Write the names of the people
they look like underneath.

Do any of the children
look like you?

FAMILY TREE

Write the names of all the people in your
family in the circles.

What did you look like when you were a baby?
Put a picture of yourself on this page.

LOOK AT US

What do you think will baby look like?

CLOTHES

Which of these clothes
do you think baby will wear?

Which would you
like to wear?

DESIGN BABY
SOME OUTFITS

Decorate these baby clothes.
Design an outfit for a party,
Halloween, a day at the beach,
a wedding....

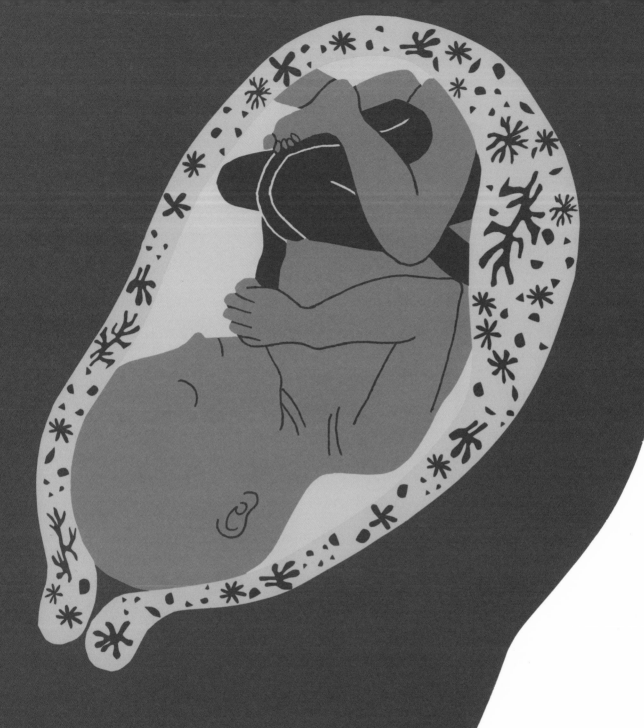

6 MONTHS

This is baby at six months.
It's about the size of a melon and
its eyes are beginning to open.

What colour are your eyes?

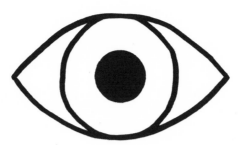 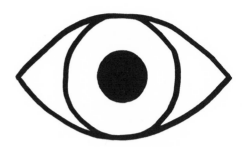

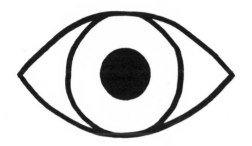 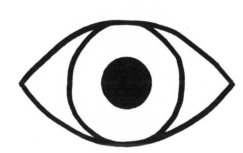

What colour are your
parents' eyes?

What colour do you think
baby's eyes will be?

The baby can hear sounds
from the outside world now.
Can you sing baby a song?

BABY BUSINESS

These are some things that mummy and daddy might need to do with baby when it first arrives.

bottle feeding

breast feeding

carrying baby

bathing baby

changing baby's diaper

At first, the baby will be too small to
play with, but you can help mummy...

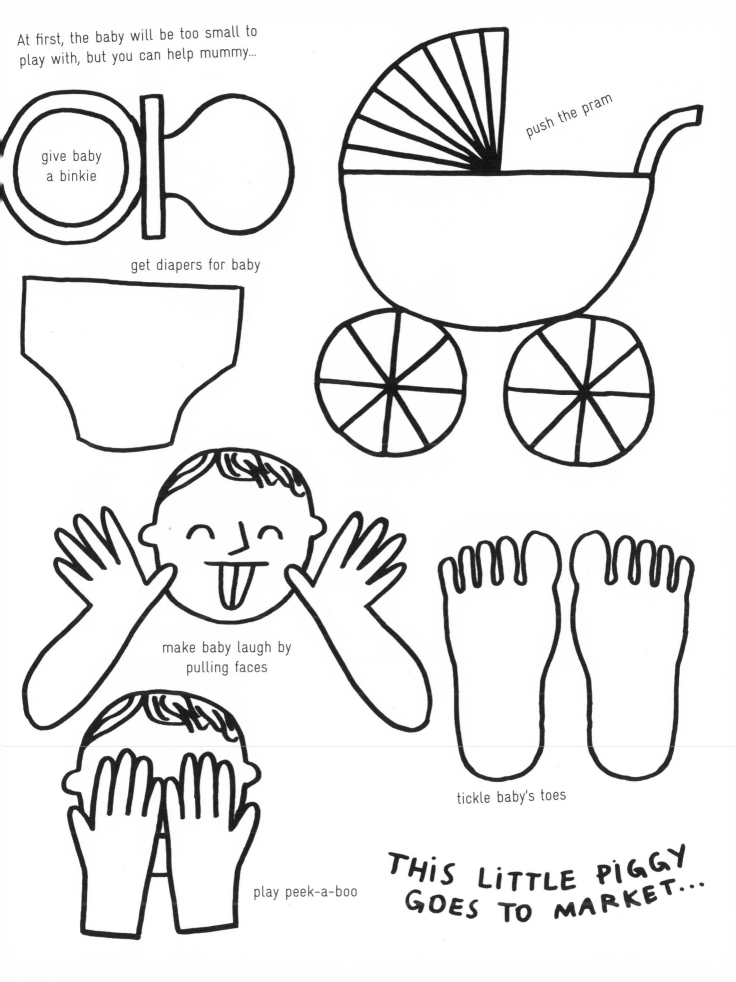

give baby
a binkie

push the pram

get diapers for baby

make baby laugh by
pulling faces

tickle baby's toes

play peek-a-boo

THIS LITTLE PIGGY
GOES TO MARKET...

HOLD
BABY

Do you think you can hold a baby? Babies' necks are a bit wobbly, so you have to remember to support their heads.

Find a doll to practice on.

Some babies like to be swaddled – wrapped up tight in their blankets.

Practice swaddling your dolly.

1

2

3

4

5

6

FOOD

Little babies can only drink milk, but you can eat all kinds of things.

What do you like to eat?

LOVE

milk

draw

COLOUR THIS PAGE IN!

write your name

I CAN

Baby can't do very much but you are big now. Can you...

kick a ball

sing a song

run really fast

clap your hands

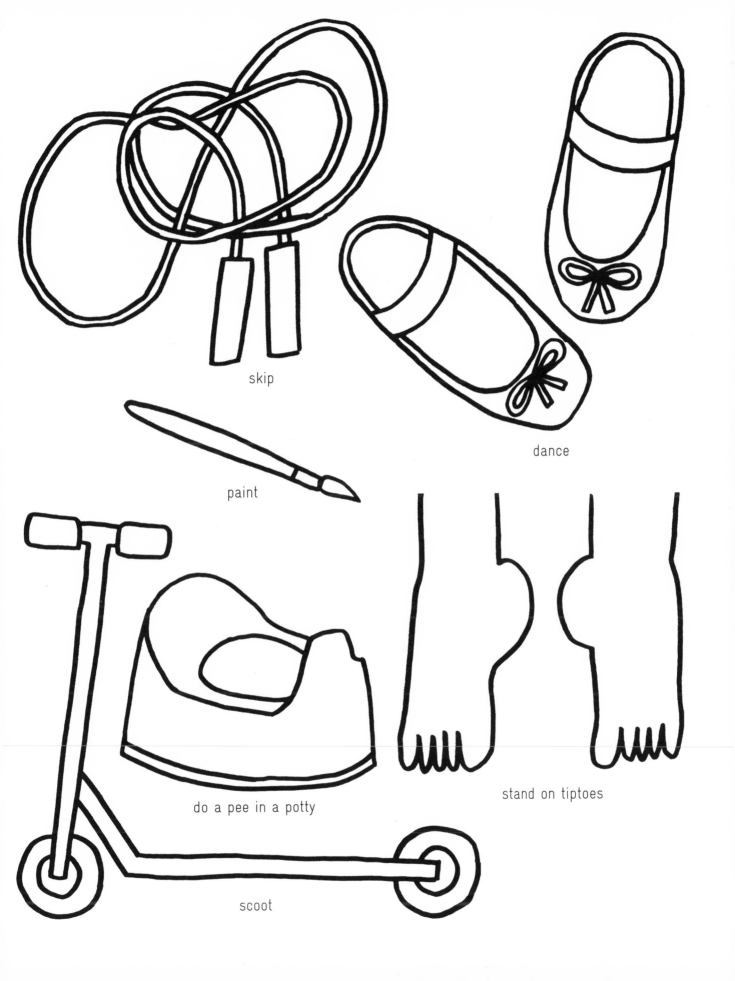

skip

paint

dance

do a pee in a potty

stand on tiptoes

scoot

SLEEP

Where will baby sleep?

THIS WAY UP ↑

STORY BOOK

What will baby sleep with?
What do you sleep with?

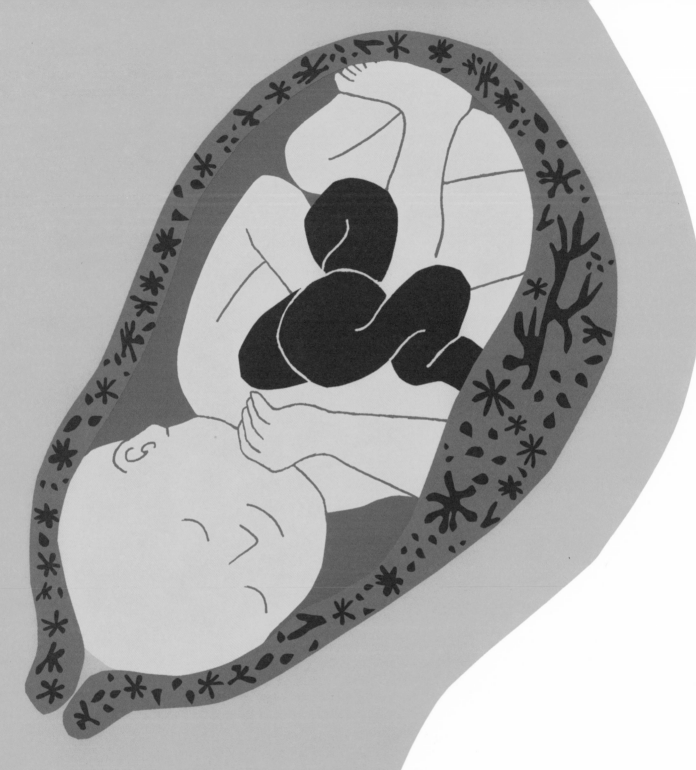

8 MONTHS

When mummy is eight months
pregnant, the baby is getting big
and chubby – it's almost the size
of a watermelon! Can you feel it
moving around and kicking?

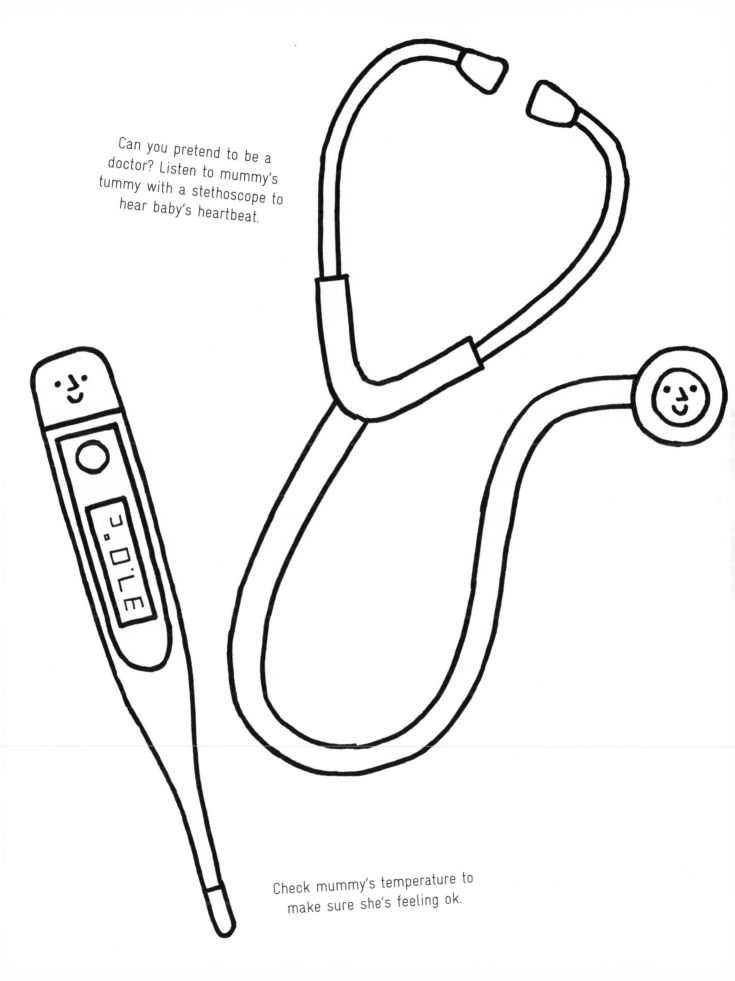

Can you pretend to be a doctor? Listen to mummy's tummy with a stethoscope to hear baby's heartbeat.

Check mummy's temperature to make sure she's feeling ok.

HOSPITAL

Mummy will probably have to go to hospital for a few days when baby arrives. She'll need to pack a bag with lots of important things.

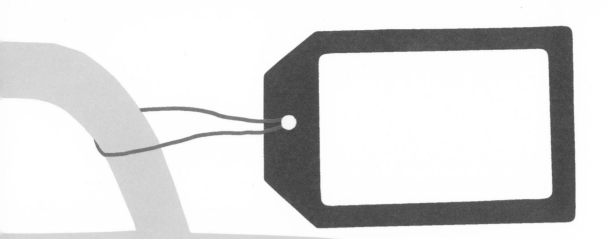

Draw some other things
she might need while she's
in hospital.

Published by Cicada Books Limited

Illustrations © Lie Dirkx
Text © Ziggy Hanaor
Design by Studio April

First published 2015 by Cicada Books Ltd. of:
48 Burghley Road, London NW5 1UE, UK

This edition published in the UK, 2020,
and the US, 2021

British Library Cataloguing-in-Publication Data.

A CIP record for this book is available from
the British Library.

ISBN: 978-1-908714-90-9

Printed in China

E: info@cicadabooks.co.uk
W: www.cicadabooks.co.uk